TRUE OR FALSE

DETERMINING WHAT WE BELIEVE AND WHY WE BELIEVE IT

OLDER WORKBOOK

Josh McDowell

Visit Tyndale's exciting Web site at www.tyndale.com

True or False Older Workbook

Some portions of this book were adapted from *Beyond Belief to Convictions*. Copyright © 2002 by Josh
McDowell, Bob Hostetler, and David H. Bellis. Used by permission of Tyndale House Publishers, Inc.,
Wheaton, Illinois 60189. All rights reserved.

Edited by Lynn Vanderzalm

Printed in the United States of America

ISBN 0-8423-8013-2

1. Undated Elective Curriculum/Middler (Grades 3 and 4)
2. Undated Elective Curriculum/Preteen (Grades 5 and 6).

TRUE OR FALSE
TABLE OF CONTENTS

All Scripture quotations are from the Holy Bible, New Living Translation (NLT)
Answers to the games, puzzles, and fill-in-the-blank activities are based on the NLT.

SESSION 1
CREATED FOR GOD

"You must worship no other gods, but only the LORD, for he is a God who is passionate about his relationship with you." Exodus 34:14

God is the Creator of the whole universe. Create means to make something from nothing. So when God created everything, he just spoke the words, and what he wanted to make appeared. But when it came to making people, God did something special. God hand-made them. He formed the first man, Adam, from the dust of the ground. He created the first woman, Eve, from Adam's rib.

People are the most important creation of God. He made us in a special way so that we could get to know him. God's plan was to create people he could love and enjoy. You see, the Bible teaches us that God is love, and more than anything, God wanted someone to love. We were created for a friendship with God. God knows that the only way we will be totally happy and enjoy our lives is when we have a friendship with him.

The world around us would like to tell us a big lie. The world says that we don't need God's friendship. Some people would rather live by their own rules and make selfish choices which they feel will make them happy. They are not interested in pleasing God.

Yes, God created you. You are special to him. God is passionate about having a friendship with you.

TODAY'S BIG TRUTH:
God created me to be his friend.

THE WORLD'S BIG LIE:
I don't need God's friendship.

Whom Do You See When You Look at You?

If I had a free day to do anything I wanted to do, I would…

_____

_____

_____.

List 5 words that describe you:

1.

2.

3.

4.

5.

What qualities would you like in a best friend?
_____
_____
_____
_____
_____

Three words that come to my mind when I think of God are:
_____
_____
_____

"Thank you for making me so wonderful-
ly complex! Your workmanship is mar-
velous—and how well I know it."
Psalm 139:14

God-People Friendships in Bible Times

Match the friends of God with the scripture:

FRIENDS OF GOD	SCRIPTURE

FRIENDS OF GOD	SCRIPTURE
Adam and Eve	Called "The friend of God." (James 2:23)
David	Jesus said, "You are my friends." (John 15:15)
Abraham	Walked with God in a garden. (Genesis 3:8–9)
Mary, Martha and Lazarus	God sent his Son as a sacrifice to take away sins. (I John 4:10)
Jesus' Disciples	Was a man after God's own heart. (Acts 13:22)
All People	The people who were standing nearby said "See how much he [Jesus] loved him." (John 11:30–36)

Thinking About Being Friends

1. What do you do to get to know your friends better?

2. How can you be a friend with God when you can't even see him?

3. How is being friends with God different from being friends with a person?

4. Tell of a time that you felt close to God.

Ways I Can Enjoy a Friendship with God

Fill in the blanks with action words that show God we believe in him.

Obey	Talk	Go to church
Worship	Read	Trust

_____ to God in prayer.
"Pray at all times" Ephesians 6:18a.

_____ God to care for me.
"Give all your worries and cares to God, for he cares about what happens to you" 1 Peter 5:7.

_____ my Bible to learn about God .
"You are my refuge and my shield; your word is my only source of hope" Psalm 119:114.

_____ God with all my heart.
"Shout with joy to the LORD, O earth! Worship the LORD with gladness. Come before him, singing with joy" Psalm 100:1–2.

_____ God's commands.
"This is my happy way of life: obeying your commandments. LORD, you are mine! I promise to obey your words!" Psalm 119:56–57.

_____ and join others in Bible study and worship.
"I was glad when they said to me, 'Let us go to the house of the LORD'" Psalm 122:1.

SESSION 2
WHAT SIN DOES TO MY FRIENDSHIP WITH GOD

**"All have turned away from God; all have gone wrong.
No one does good, not even one." Romans 3:12**

The Good News is that God wants to be our friend! The sad truth is that because of sin, we have broken our friendship with God. So how did sin enter into the perfect world God created for Adam and Eve?

God gave Adam and Eve a wonderful gift. It was the ability to make the choice to obey God. None of the animals or anything else God made had that wonderful choice. God gave Adam and Eve just one rule to live by. All they had to do was to show God how much they loved him by choosing to obey his one rule. One sad day, Adam and Eve chose to disobey God. Choosing to disobey God is called sin. God is holy, which means he is pure and perfect in every way.

Because God loves us so much he has given us rules in the Bible that will help us live in ways which please him. These rules will make our life happier and so much better. God knows the best thing for us to do is choose to obey him. The world, however, has a sad big lie for us. It says that we can each decide for ourselves what is right or wrong for us. We often get tempted to think that what is right or wrong really depends on what is happening or what we think would be the best thing to do at the moment. But what God says is more important than what we think.

TODAY'S BIG TRUTH:
God is holy and takes my sin seriously.

THE WORLD'S BIG LIE:
I can decide what is right or wrong for me.

True or False

As a Result of Sin...

Read the scriptures and discover what happened as a result of sin.

Before Man Sinned

1. Adam had a beautiful garden in which to work.

2. Adam's work was a pleasurable pastime.

3. Eve was to be joyfully blessed with children.

4. The serpent had legs.

5. Adam and Eve lived in the Garden of Eden.

As a Result of Sin

1. A _____ was placed on the _____ . The land would grow _____ and _____ . (Genesis 3:17–18)

2. Adam would have to _____ to make a _____ . (Genesis 3:17)

3. Though Eve would still have children, and childbearing would still bring her joy, it would also bring _____ . (Genesis 3:16)

4. The serpent would grovel in the _____ and _____ on his _____ . (Genesis 3:14)

5. God _____ them from the garden. (Genesis 3:23)

I Can Choose To Agree With God

Because you know God wants to be your close friend, how do you want to act when you are confronted by a temptation to sin? Match the three Bible verses with the three statements below.

I agree with God that sin hurts me when I...

"Above all else, guard your heart, for it affects everything you do."
Proverbs 4:23

Decide to follow God and to resist evil.

"Pursue faith and love and peace, and enjoy the companionship of those who call on the Lord with pure hearts."
2 Timothy 2:22

Know and act on God's commands.

"I have hidden your word in my heart that I might not sin against you."
Psalm 119:11

Pick friends who will help me avoid evil and choose good.

Think of a real temptation you face and tell how one of the verses above will help you to choose God's way the next time you are tempted.

_____

_____

_____

Help Wanted

The following kids need your help. Each of them has chosen to believe one of the World's Big Lies, "I can decide what is right or wrong for me." How would you advise them?

1. Brandon is a very smart student. He always makes A's in school. He has developed the attitude that he is always right. Recently, he accused Bill of taking his spelling book. He really made Bill feel bad, and he talked about it to everyone in the classroom. Even though Bill promised he had not even seen Brandon's book, everyone thought he had it. That night, Brandon found his spelling book in his own bedroom.

   The next day, Brandon did not say anything about it. He thought it would make him look bad if he told Bill and the others the truth, that he had left his spelling book at home.

   What was Brandon's problem? _____

   If Brandon believed that God takes sin seriously, what should he do?

   _____

   _____

   _____

2. Melissa goes to church every Sunday. She has learned that God loves her. She feels that she is special to God. Last week she turned 10 years old. She and a few friends were going to the city zoo. Her mother had given her $20 to pay for her admission to the zoo and to have extra spending money. At the gate she saw that the children under 10 only had to pay $2, while those 10 and over had to pay $5 to get in. She knew most of her girlfriends had not turned 10 yet, so it would not be a problem for her to quietly tell the attendant she was under 10. Then she could have an extra $3 to spend. After all, the Bible teaches us that God wants to forgive us of all our sins.

   What was Melissa's problem? _____

If Melissa believed that sin would hurt her friendship with God, what should she do?

_____

_____

3. Joshua was at the video/DVD store with his older brother. He saw two DVDs which he really wanted, but only had money for one. He had both of them in his hands. He remembered that his jacket had an inside pocket. He thought, "If I pay for one, the store will still get its money; after all they probably get these at half price." Anyway, it is not like he was stealing something really big. It was just $14. The store would not miss it. After all, just think of all the big sins people commit every day. This is just a little one.

What was Joshua's problem? _____

If Joshua really believed that God was holy and he wanted to please God, what should he do?

_____

_____

4. Michelle loved to talk. She was one of those people who knew something about everyone. When she heard about something bad about someone, she could hardly wait to tell somebody. She never bothered to check out the story to see if it was true. And so what if it was not; she was just passing on what she had heard.

What was Michelle's problem? _____

If Michelle really wanted to please God, what would you tell her she should do?

_____

_____

True or False

SESSION 3
LOST AND ALONE BECAUSE OF SIN

"For all have sinned; all fall short of God's glorious standard." Romans 3:23

"For the wages of sin is death, but the free gift of God is eternal life through Christ Jesus our Lord." Romans 6:23

Today we are going to learn how sin affects us.

We are all tempted to sin. Sometimes we disobey God because it just seems to be the easiest thing to do at the moment. There are other times that we sin because we want other kids to like us. There are even times that we sin because we think we can get by with it. No matter why we have made the wrong choice, sin always leaves us feeling lost and alone—away from God.

Some people think, "Well, it's my life; I can choose what I want to do. This bad attitude says that what God wants for us is not important. There is a selfishness deep in our hearts that makes us want to do things our own way. This selfish attitude is resistance toward God.

The first step in making things right with God is to:

- Admit to God that you have sinned.
- Ask God to forgive you of your sin.
- Look for ways to resist sin. God promises to always provide us an escape when we are tempted to sin.

TODAY'S BIG TRUTH:
Sin separates me from God

THE WORLD'S BIG LIE:
I can live my life my way.

True or False

The Truth About Sin

"If we say we have no sin, we are only fooling ourselves and refusing to accept the truth." 1 John 1:8

Sin separates us from God. But what exactly is sin? What makes sin wrong?

1. An action isn't a sin if you don't feel bad when you do it
   (see Romans 3:23). True or False

   Why? _____

   _____

2. There are some really good people like grandparents and pastors who
   have never committed a sin
   (see Romans 3:23). True or False

   Why? _____

   _____

3. Little sins like "white lies" are no big deal to God
   (see James 2:19). True or False

   Why? _____

   _____

4. I'm not so bad; lots of people are bigger sinners than I am
   (see Romans 3:12). True or False

   Why? _____

   _____

5. If I can do a lot of good things, I can make up for the bad things I do
   (see Ephesians 2:9). True or False

   Why? _____

Choose To Obey God's Ways

Crossword Puzzle

DOWN:

1. Tell the truth, do not _lie._

2. Pay for what you take from a store, do not _____.

3. Control your _____ when you get angry.

7. Study hard so that you will not be tempted to _____ in school.

8. Avoid _____ which displease God because he cares about what you see.

9. Learn to tell clean jokes and not _____ ones.

10. Respect your body and do not do _____.

ACROSS:

4. Treat other kids with respect. Do not kick or _____ them.

5. Obey your parents and do not _____ them.

6. Speak kindly of others, do not _____.

Escape!

"But remember that the temptations that come into your life are no different from what others experience. And God is faithful. He will keep the temptation from becoming so strong that you can't stand up against it. When you are tempted, he will show you a way out so that you will not give in to it." 1 Corinthians 10:13

Can you help Randy, Kim, and Carlos think of ways they can escape their temptations? All three of these kids go to church and will tell you they love Jesus, but they are each tempted to do what they know they should not do.

1. Randy has great friends at church, but only one of them is in his class at school. He is very outgoing and likes to be in the "in" crowd. The one boy in his class at both school and church is not really in with the cool kids. When Randy is with his church friends, he does okay, but he is unsure of himself with his school friends. He really wants to impress his school friends by being cool. The guys in the group he runs with often tell jokes which make him feel uncomfortable. He knows that the words they are saying displease God and would not please his parents, but he really wants to hang around and hear the jokes. He is so afraid of what the other guys would think if they knew how he felt, so he tries to laugh and play along. It is just so tempting to join in.

   What is Randy's way of escape? _____

   _____

   _____

2. Kim is smart and can make good grades. She really likes to study and always wants to make A's. She becomes upset if she gets a B. One day, while helping her teacher, she found the place where the teacher kept the test which she was planning to give on Friday. Kim slipped a copy of the test out quickly, and she was able to study with it. When she took the test in class, it was very easy for her because she had already worked

it out. When she got a perfect score and then got by with it, she was thrilled. Unfortunately, she has developed a habit of snooping around the teacher's desk and watching carefully where the teacher puts things. Taking another test almost seems like a game. It would be so tempting.

What is Kim's way of escape? _____

_____

_____

3. Carlos really loves his parents very much, but he thinks they have too many rules for him. His parents pay for his school lunches ahead of time so he will not have to carry money to school each day. This is also a way they can be sure he gets the whole meal and does not spend his lunch money on the soft drinks and junk food in vending machines. Deep down inside Carlos knows his parents are doing the right thing, but he wants the stuff some of his friends are eating. He has thought of talking to his parents about his feelings, but then he discovered a large jar where his parents drop change in their bedroom closet. Carlos is careful to not get caught, but daily for the last two weeks he has been able to buy something from the vending machines. He knows he should stop doing this, but it is just too tempting.

What is Carlos's way of escape?_____

_____

_____

True or False

SESSION 4

JESUS IS THE ONE AND ONLY SAVIOR

"Jesus told him, I am the way, the truth, and the life. No one can come to the Father except through me." John 14:6

There are some people who believe there are a lot of ways to get to know God. Some believe that everyone worships the same God, but they may just use different names for God. But Jesus said he is the Son of the one true God.

God sent Jesus to be the Savior of the world. Jesus said that there is no other way to know God except through him. That is why it is so important to memorize our Bible verse today. It will always remind us of Jesus' words, that he is the way to God, he is the truth about God, and he is the only way to live in friendship with God forever.

We can recognize that Jesus is the Savior through the many signs that were foretold about him. These signs are called prophecies. Hundreds of years before Jesus was ever born, men who spoke for God gave us signs that God would send a Savior to forgive us of sin. Even though there are more than three hundred signs, each one can be seen in Jesus!

Jesus did miracles that only God could do. Each of the miracles also shows us that Jesus is God. But the greatest miracle of all was when Jesus came back from the dead.

TODAY'S BIG TRUTH:
God sent Jesus to be the Savior of the world.

THE WORLD'S BIG LIE:
There are a lot of ways to get to know God.

Only One God, Only One Savior

Look up the verse in your Bible and fill in the blanks with the right word.

1. Isaiah 45:5

"I am the LORD: _____ _____ _____ _____ _____."

2. John 14:6

"Jesus told him, 'I am the _____, the _____, and the _____.

_____ _____ can come to the Father except through _____.'"

3. Acts 4:12

"There   is   <u>salvation</u>   in   _____ _____   else!   There   is

_____ _____ <u>name</u> in all of <u>heaven</u> for people to call

on to save them."

4. 1 John 4:9

"God _____ how much he loved us by sending his

_____ _____ into the world so that we might

have eternal life through him."

Three-Way Prophecy Match
Facts About Jesus

More than 400 years before Jesus was born, Old Testament Bible writers spoke about Jesus. They told of the future details of his life so that when Jesus came people would know he was the Son of God. Look up the New Testament verses and place them in the right blank under "Prophecy Fulfilled."

NEW TESTAMENT VERSES
Matthew 2:1; Matthew 9:35;
Matthew 26:49; Luke 3:23–31; Acts 2:31

FACTS ABOUT JESUS	OLD TESTAMENT PROPHECY	NEW TESTAMENT PROPHECY FULFILLED
Jesus would be a descendent of King David.	Jeremiah 23:5	_____
Jesus would be born in Bethlehem.	Micah 5:2	_____
Jesus would perform many miracles.	Isaiah 35:5–6	_____
Jesus would be betrayed by a friend.	Psalm 41:9	_____
Jesus would be raised from the dead the third day after his death.	Psalm 16:10	_____

SESSION 5
I CAN BE FORGIVEN

"For God sent Jesus to take the punishment for our sins and to satisfy God's anger against us. We are made right with God when we believe that Jesus shed his blood, sacrificing his life for us. God was being entirely fair and just when he did not punish those who had sinned in former times."
Romans 3:25

The best news you will ever hear is that you can be forgiven of your sin. God wants to be your friend, but your sin separates you from God. The wrong things you do break God's laws and hurt the people God loves. It breaks God's heart that your sin has separated you from him. Your sin is the problem.

God solved our problem with sin through Jesus' death on the cross. God accepts Jesus' death as the payment for all our sins. There is nothing that you or I can do to earn our own way into heaven or gain a friendship with God.

You can be forgiven by trusting that Jesus died for you. You can ask God to forgive you and he will because Jesus paid for your sins with his own life. By trusting in Jesus as your Savior you will have a friendship with God forever.

TODAY'S BIG TRUTH:
God planned for Jesus to pay the price for my sins.

TODAY'S BIG LIE:
I am a good person—I can please God.

True or False

Why Jesus Died For Me

Decide if each of the statements is true or false.

TRUE OR FALSE?

1. God loves me even though I have sinned.

   T/ F

2. If I am extra good, I will be good enough to be God's friend.

   T/ F

3. My dad and mom are Christians so God will let me into heaven too.

   T/ F

4. When Jesus died on the cross, he was dying for my sin.

   T/ F

5. If I just say to myself I'm sorry for doing wrong, I will be forgiven.

   T/ F

6. Doing good things earns me a place in heaven.

   T/ F

7. The only way to become God's friend is by trusting Jesus as the one who paid the price for my sins.

   T/ F

8. All people who try hard to be good and are sincere about whatever they believe will go to heaven.

   T/ F

WHY?   WHAT DOES THE BIBLE SAY?

Romans 5:8 says, "But God showed his great love for us by sending Christ to die for us while we were still sinners."

Romans 3:12 says, "All have turned away from God; all have gone wrong. No one does good, not even one."

2 Corinthians 5:10 says, "For we must all stand before Christ to be judged. We will each receive whatever we deserve for the good or evil we have done in our bodies."

1 Peter 3:18 says, "Christ also suffered when he died for our sins once for all time. He never sinned, but he died for sinners that he might bring us safely home to God. He suffered physical death, but he was raised to life in the Spirit."

John 6:29 says, "Jesus told them, 'This is what God wants you to do: Believe in the one he has sent.'"

Ephesians 2:9 says, "Salvation is not a reward for the good things we have done, so none of us can boast about it."

Roman 3: 22–23 says, "We are made right in God's sight when we trust in Jesus Christ to take away our sins. And we all can be saved in this same way, no matter who we are or what we have done. For all have sinned; all fall short of God's glorious standard."

Acts 4:12 says, "There is salvation in no one else! There is no other name in all of heaven for people to call on to save them."

Admitting to Sin

"So he returned home to his father. And while he was still a long distance away, his father saw him coming. Filled with love and compassion, he ran to his son, embraced him, and kissed him. His son said to him, 'Father, I have sinned against both heaven and you, and I am no longer worthy of being called your son.' But his father said to the servants, 'Quick! Bring the finest robe in the house and put it on him. Get a ring for his finger, and sandals for his feet.'" Luke 15:20–22

1. What did the lost son do right?

_____

_____

2. Is it hard to admit it when you are wrong?

_____

_____

3. Why?

_____

_____

4. How did the father in this story respond to his son who was lost?

_____

_____

5. How do you think God our heavenly Father will respond to us when we seek his forgiveness?

_____

_____

Admitting that we were wrong is the first step in having a friendship with God.

Forgiveness Feels Good!

Read the following Bible passages.
1. Circle every word that describes a good feeling.
2. Draw a square around each word that describes a bad feeling.

Psalm 32:1–5

"Oh, what joy for those

whose rebellion is forgiven,

whose sin is put out of sight!

Yes, what joy for those

whose record the LORD has cleared of sin,

whose lives are lived in complete honesty!

When I refused to confess my sin.

I was weak and miserable,

and I groaned all day long.

Day and night your hand of discipline was heavy on me.

My strength evaporated like water in the summer heat.

Finally, I confessed all my sins to you

and stopped trying to hide them.

I said to myself, "I will confess my rebellion to the LORD."

And you forgave me! All my guilt is gone."

What brought joy to the writer of this psalm? _____

_____

_____

SESSION 6

I CAN BE SURE JESUS WILL ALWAYS LOVE ME

"I assure you, those who listen to my message and believe in God who sent me have eternal life. They will never be condemned for their sins, but they have already passed from death into life." John 5:24

Did you know that God loves you just like you are? It is true. There is nothing that you can do to make God love you more.

Jesus wants to always love you. We begin a special friendship with God the very day we ask him to forgive us of our sin. That friendship is to last forever. The Bible teaches us that there is nothing that can separate us from God's love. There are some people who want us to believe that we have to work hard to please God in our own power.

Incarnation is a big word we will learn about today. It means "in the flesh." Jesus, who had always lived in heaven, came to this earth "in the flesh"—he became a person with skin on! He did this because he wanted to let us get to know him so we can deepen our friendship.

TODAY'S BIG TRUTH:
Jesus will never leave me.

THE WORLD'S BIG LIE:
I must work hard to please God on my own.

HEAVEN IS A FREE GIFT

Draw a picture of what you look forward to seeing in heaven.

"I assure you, those who listen to my message and believe in
God who sent me have eternal life." John 5:24

The Facts About Feelings

Word Search

Directions: Find these twelve words in the word search box below.

Happy	Tired	Sad	Thrilled
Cranky	Glad	Fine	Joyful
Sick	Sleepy	Excited	Disappointed

```
S  D  E  T  N  I  O  P  P  A  S  I  D
H  U  P  E  R  S  R  T  Y  U  I  O  P
A  N  C  P  K  G  L  A  D  S  A  Q  E
L  O  K  I  P  H  G  E  D  F  G  H  J
D  U  C  R  T  U  R  V  E  B  N  K  H
E  N  I  F  U  I  R  F  R  P  T  J  A
L  J  S  P  Y  T  S  P  F  N  Y  O  P
L  D  J  T  I  R  E  D  P  Y  T  P  P
I  C  O  R  Y  E  P  C  R  A  N  K  Y
R  F  Y  E  N  T  K  U  P  K  G  L  A
H  G  F  E  X  C  I  T  E  D  S  T  U
T  Y  U  C  I  A  C  J  P  U  C  A  R
N  O  L  R  P  H  B  Y  Z  B  O  G  D
```

The facts about feelings are:
- Feelings are a part of being a person.
- Our feelings change due to what is happening right now.
- Our feelings can be affected by everything from our health to the weather.
- Feelings are wonderful and make life exciting, but they cannot always be trusted.
- There may be times we feel unsure that Jesus will always love us. At those times, we should trust God's promises in the Bible. John 5:24 says, "I assure you, those who listen to my message and believe in God who sent me have eternal life."

I Can Be Sure

What happens when a person becomes a Christian?
Read over the ten statements and cross out the ones that aren't <u>totally</u>
and <u>always</u> true. Match the four statements that are left with the four
Bible verses which teach us that the statement is true.

When I become a Christian...

1. I will only have happy feelings all the time.

2. I have a home waiting for me in heaven.

3. I have the right to live like I want.

4. I have eternal life.

5. I become a new person.

6. I stop being tempted to sin.

7. I instantly get the whole Bible downloaded into my brain.

8. I can pray beautiful prayers aloud so other people can know I'm a Christian.

9. I become God's child.

10. I automatically have perfect attendance in Sunday school.

Bible Verses:

A. "I assure you, those who listen to my message and believe in God who sent me have eternal life. They will never be condemned for their sins, but they have already passed from death into life." John 5:24

B. "But to all who believed him and accepted him, he gave the right to become children of God." John 1:12

C. "What this means is that those who become Christians become new persons. They are not the same anymore, for the old life is gone. A new life has begun!" 2 Corinthians 5:17

D. "There are many rooms in my Father's home, and I am going to prepare a place for you. If this were not so, I would tell you plainly." John 14:2

SESSION 7
GROWING UP IN GOD'S FAMILY

"But to all who believed him and accepted him, he gave the right to become the children of God." John 1:12

God wants us to be more than just friends. He wants to be a part of every hour of every day in our lives. He wants us to be a part of his family. John 1:12 tells us that when we trust in Jesus, we become God's children.

We all want to have someone who understands us. God made us, so he knows us perfectly. Jesus came to earth and lived as a real person. He really knows how it feels to grow up in a world like ours. Did you know that at one time Jesus was your very age?

God wants us in his family forever. As long as we live here on earth, we can continue to learn more about God. We can pray to him and know that he wants to meet our needs, just like any loving father would want to do for his children. Jesus said that he would prepare a place for us in heaven so that we could be in his family forever.

TODAY'S BIG TRUTH:
When I trust in Jesus, God makes me his child.

THE WORLD'S BIG LIE:
God and the church are fine—when I have the time.

CHILDREN'S RIGHTS

*"But to all who believed him and accepted him, he gave the right
to become the children of God." John 1:12*

When we trust in Jesus, God the Father makes us his child. Can you think of at least
five things you will receive from God because you are his child?

1. _____

2. _____

3. _____

4. _____

5. _____

Write a thank-you prayer to God for what you have listed.

Dear heavenly Father,

_____

_____

_____

_____

_____

_____

Love,

_____

GOD UNDERSTANDS

"That is why we have a great High Priest who has gone to heaven, Jesus the Son of God. Let us cling to him and never stop trusting him. This High Priest of ours understands our weaknesses, for he faced all the same temptations we do, yet he did not sin. So let us come boldly before the throne of our gracious God. There we will receive his mercy, and we will find grace to help us when we need it." Hebrews 4:14-16

This verse says that Jesus understands our _____

Why? _____

_____

But Jesus never _____

So we can come _____
.

When we talk to God we will receive:

1. _____

2. _____

I need Jesus to understand and help me with

_____

_____

_____

Can You Help?

Check out these case studies. Write your answers in the blanks.

JESSICA

Jessica got all her homework done early and played with her friends until suppertime. After supper she stayed on the phone until time for her bath and bedtime. Was she ever tired! Her dad came by her room and said, "Jessica, have you read your Bible and devotion for today?" Oops! She knew she had not. Jessica thinks, *Can't God understand I'm tired?*

What should Jessica do? _____

_____

Why? _____

_____

COLIN

Colin has a best friend he likes to spend time with. Colin's family is faithful to attend church, but his friend's family does not have a church. They plan the coolest things to do on Sundays and often invite Colin to go along. At first Colin did not ask his parents if he could go; he just thought they would say no. But now he is wondering why he could not go at least once a month.

What should Colin do?_____

_____

Why? _____

_____

SARAH

Sarah loves to just stay at home. She likes to read, cook, sleep late, and play with her toys. This Sunday morning her mother walked into her room and told her it was time to get up and get ready for church. Her grandparents called and are pick-ing her up. Sarah doesn't feel like getting out of bed. *Anyway*, she thinks, *my parents stay home, so why do I need to go to church?*

What should Sarah do? _____

_____

Why? _____

_____

SESSION 8
CELEBRATE!
A Son Returns and a Father Celebrates

To illustrate the point further, Jesus told them this story: "A man had two sons. The younger son told his father, 'I want my share of your estate now instead of waiting until you die.'" So his father agreed to divide his wealth between his sons.

"A few days later this younger son packed all his belongings and took a trip to a distant land, and there he wasted all his money on wild living. About the time his money ran out, a great famine swept over the land, and he began to starve. He persuaded a local farmer to hire him to feed his pigs. The boy became so hungry that even the pods he was feeding the pigs looked good to him. But no one gave him anything."

"When he finally came to his senses, he said to himself, 'At home even the hired men have food enough to spare, and here I am, dying of hunger! I will go home to my father and say, "Father, I have sinned against both heaven and you, and I am no longer worthy of being called your son. Please take me on as a hired man."

"So he returned home to his father. And while he was still a long distance away, his father saw him coming. Filled with love and compassion, he ran to his son, embraced him, and kissed him. His son said to him, 'Father I have sinned against both heaven and you, and I am no longer worthy of being called your son.'"

"But his father said to the servants, 'Quick! Bring the finest robe in the house and put it on him. Get a ring for his finger, and sandals for his feet. And kill the calf we have been fattening in the pen. We must celebrate with a feast, for this son of mine was dead and has now returned to life. He was lost, but now he is found.'" So the party began.

Luke 15:11–24

TODAY'S BIG TRUTH:
God celebrates when I come back to him.

True or False

THE FATHER CELEBRATES

Narrator 1:   You are about to hear a love story. It's about the love God has for us as his creation and everything God did to have a friendship with us.

Narrator 2:   Our story is wrapped around a Bible passage you probably know as the parable of the Lost Son.

All Kids: We were CREATED FOR GOD.

Child 1:   "So God created people in his own image; God patterned them after himself; male and female he created them" (Genesis 1:27).

Narrator 1:   In the very beginning, God created everything. He made a perfect place for people to live and called it the Garden of Eden. They had everything they needed.

Narrator 2:   There Adam and Eve lived and enjoyed their friendship with God. They talked to him like they talked to each other. They walked with him in the Garden. They laughed together and enjoyed the beautiful trees, flowers and playful animals.

Narrator 1:   Adam and Eve enjoyed God's love. They were joyful. They were at peace.

Narrator 2:   God enjoyed Adam and Eve. He was glad he created them. He loved them very much.

All Kids: The Big Truth is, **God created me to be his friend.** *(Children should stand up and clasp their hands together, like a handshake.)*

All Kids: "You must worship no other gods, but only the LORD, for he is a God who is passionate about his relationship with you" (Exodus 34:14).

Narrator 1:   God is passionate about his friendship with us! What a thrilling thought that the God who created the whole universe cares for me and wants my friendship.

Narrator 2:   If only life had stayed that simple. But one sad day, Adam and Eve chose to disobey God. God gave them just one rule, and they disobeyed that rule. Disobedience to God is called sin.

All Kids: SIN DESTROYS MY FRIENDSHIP WITH GOD.

Narrator 1:   Jesus once told a story about a man who had two sons. The younger son told his father…

Son: I want my share of your estate now, instead of waiting until you die.

Narrator 2:   *(Father pantomimes this action.)* So his father agreed to divide his wealth between his sons.

Narrator 1:   When the son asked for his father's money, he was saying, "Father, I want nothing to do with you. I don't want you as my father. In fact, I wish you were dead."

Narrator 2:   The son took the money and ran away from home.

Narrator 1:   We are all like that son in the story. We have all run away from God, our father. We've run away from God, our greatest friend. We did that by failing to keep God's rules about loving him and others.

All Kids: "All have turned away from God; all have gone wrong. No one does good, not even one" (Romans 3:12).

Child 1:   We disobey our parents.

Child 2:   We fight with our brothers and sisters.

Child 3:   We don't share and refuse to help others.

Child 4:   We lie and steal.

Child 5:   We cheat in school and at games.

Child 6:   We speak unkind and often bad words.

Child 7:   We do not trust Jesus to forgive us of our sin.

Child 8:   We run away from our Father God.

True or False

Narrator 2: Sin hurts us. It hurts other people. And it breaks God's heart. God wants to be friends with each of us. But the wrong things we do make it impossible for us to be God's friends.

Child 2: Habakkuk 1:13 says, "Your eyes are too pure to look on evil; you cannot tolerate wrong. (NIV)"

Narrator 1: God is holy, which means he never does wrong. But when we choose to do wrong things, we turn away from him. That breaks God's heart, because he wants our friendship. That's why our sin is such a big deal to God.

All Kids: The Big Truth is, **God is holy and takes my sin seriously.**
(*Cross arms in front of face.*)

Narrator 2: Sin leaves us feeling lost and alone and away from God.

All Kids: We are LOST AND ALONE BECAUSE OF SIN.

Narrator 1: We all have the very same problem. We have all failed God.

All Kids: "For all have sinned; all fall short of God's glorious standard" (Romans 3:23).

Narrator 2: Remember the lost son? He was secure while he lived with his father. Listen to what happened to him when he ran away from his father.

Narrator 1: (*Son acts this out as it is read.*) A few days later this younger son packed all his belongings and took a trip to a distant land, and there he wasted all his money on wild living. About the time his money ran out, a great famine swept over the land, and he began to starve. He persuaded a local farmer to hire him to feed his pigs. The boy became so hungry that even the pods he was feeding the pigs looked good to him. But no one gave him anything.

Narrator 2: Sin creates a huge problem between God and us. God says that when we sin, we are lost and alone. Sin takes us far away from God. It sep–arates us from him. Let's act out what it means to be separated from God.

Act out with "all kids" the demonstration from session 3. Have one adult in the middle wearing sign that says "God." All kids should gather closely around him or her—in a group hug. Ask: "How close are we now?" (They should answer, very close or all together.) Have everyone take one step back. Say: "That's what happens to us when we sin." Step back again. Say: "Each time we sin, we get further and further away from God. None of us can reach him. We can't reach each other." Keep taking one step back until no one can stretch a hand out to "God" or to anyone else.

All Kids: The Big Truth is, **Sin separates me from God.**
(With arms extended forward palms out with fingers pointed upward, take two steps back, as if pushing away.)

Narrator 1: When we sin, we are separated from God. No one else can rescue us—not our friends, not our parents, not our pastor, not any human being. And there's nothing we can do to rescue ourselves. The wrong things we do have taken us so far away that we are lost and alone and can't find our way back to God.

Narrator 2: The Bible calls that painful kind of separation "death." When someone's body dies, we're completely cut off from that person. That's physical death. But there's another kind of death that is even worse. "Spiritual death" is when people are far from God.

All Kids: "For the wages of sin is death" (Romans 6:23).

Narrator 2: Separation from God is the result of sin. That sounds bad—and it is.

Narrator 1: We're lost and alone. Who is going to help us?

All Kids: JESUS IS THE ONE AND ONLY SAVIOR.

Narrator 2: Acts 4:12 tells us that Jesus is the only one who can save us. His name is the only power in the world that has been given to redeem his lost and alone people. He is our only hope.

All Kids: Jesus says, "I am the way, the truth, and the life. No one can come to the Father except through me" (John 14:6).

True or False

Narrator 1: God wanted us to be able to recognize the one he sent to save us. So God gave us three special ways to be sure that Jesus is the world's one-and-only Savior.

Child 3: Because Jesus fulfilled hundreds of Old Testament prophecies, we could be sure he was born to be our Savior.

Child 4: Because Jesus performed miracles, we could be sure he was God in the flesh.

Child 5: Because Jesus rose from the dead, we could be sure he was God's chosen One—and that he had paid for our sins in full.

Narrator 2: Some people say there are lots of ways to be friends with God. But Jesus is the world's one-and-only Savior.

All Kids: The Big Truth is, **God sent Jesus to be the Savior of the world.** (*Touch palm of each hand alternately with the middle finger, as the sign language symbol for Jesus, then point to heaven with the right hand.*)

Narrator 1: Remember the lost son? Well, he finally came to his senses. He said to himself,

Lost Son: At home even the hired men have food enough to spare, and here I am, dying of hunger! I will go home to my father and say, "Father, I have sinned against both heaven and you, and I am no longer worthy of being called your son. Please take me on as a hired man."

Narrator 2: The lost son did a really smart thing. He recognized that there was one place he could get help—his father. He needed to be forgiven for running away from his father. Would his father help him? Would his father forgive him? Can we be forgiven?

All Kids: I CAN BE FORGIVEN!

Narrator 1: Our heavenly Father wants us to recognize that there is only one place we can get help. God has a plan to bring us to himself and make us friends with him.

All Kids: The Big Truth is, **God sent Jesus to pay the price for my sin.** (*Cross hands over face, then break arms apart and reach up to God as a child wanting to be held.*)

Narrator 1: If we want to be friends with God, our sin must be dealt with. And we can't do that ourselves. There's only one way to do it. When Jesus died on the cross, he died for all of our sin. He did something we can't do. Only Jesus could pay the price for our sin, and that's exactly what Jesus did.

All Kids: "For God sent Jesus to take the punishment for our sins and to satisfy God's anger against us. We are made right with God when we believe that Jesus shed his blood, sacrificing his life for us" Romans 3:25.

Narrator 2: The death of Jesus on the cross makes it possible for us to be friends of God.

Child 6: Romans 5:8 says, "But God showed his great love for us by sending Christ to die for us while we were still sinners."

Narrator 2: That's good news. But our lost son is still stuck with the pigs. What about him?

Narrator 1: The lost son returned home to his father. And while he was still a long distance away, his father saw him coming. Filled with love and compassion, he ran to his son, embraced him, and kissed him. His son said to him,

Lost Son: Father, I have sinned against both heaven and you, and I am no longer worthy of being called your son.

Narrator 2: The son ran home to his father.

Narrator 1: God wants us to run home to him by trusting in the death of Jesus for the forgiveness of our sins. And when we do, God comes running to us.

Narrator 2: We cannot save ourselves from our sin and become friends with God by anything we do.

Narrator 1: We need a miracle to happen–and that's exactly what God does. God performs a miracle that will last forever.

All Kids: I CAN BE SURE JESUS WILL ALWAYS LOVE ME.

Narrator 2: There is nothing that I can do that will cause Jesus to love me more.

All Kids: The Big Truth is, **Jesus will never leave me.**
(Hug self with arms wrapped around.)

Narrator 1: We have a friendship with God because we have faith in Jesus. We will live forever in heaven because Jesus will never leave us.

All Kids: Jesus said, "I assure you, those who listen to my message and believe in God who sent me have eternal life" (John 5:24).

Narrator 2: When we trust in Jesus, and God is our Father, we have a new, big family.

All Kids: It is so much fun to be GROWING UP IN GOD'S FAMILY.

Child 7: God my Father understands me, and he understands you!

Child 8: God my Father will love me always!

All Kids: The Big Truth is: **When I trust in Jesus, God makes me his child.**
(Form arms as if rocking a baby.)

Narrator 1: God doesn't just want us to be his friends; he wants us to be a part of his family. We become God's son or daughter.

All Kids: "But to all who believed him and accepted him, he gave the right to become children of God" (John 1:12).

Narrator 2: There is another Big Truth to this wonderful story.

Narrator 1: Let's hear the Father tell us in his own words!

Father: *(Say to the servants,)* Quick! Bring the finest robe in the house and put it on him. Get a ring for his finger, and sandals for his feet. And kill the calf we have been fattening in the pen. We must celebrate with a feast, for this son of mine was dead and has now returned to life. He was lost, but now he is found.

All Kids: The Big Truth is, **God celebrates when I come back to him!**
(Clap hands; then raise arms, palms up.)

Narrator 1:   So the party began.

Narrator 2:   That's exactly what God does for us when we trust in Christ. He cele-brates. We were lost, but now we are found. We were dead but are now alive. We were his enemy, but now we are his friends, and we will live together with God and his people in heaven forever.

Narrator 1:   Let's hear those Big Truths again:

All kids: (Say the eight Big Truths in unison with the motions.)
1. God created me to be his friend.

2. God is holy and takes my sin seriously.

3. Sin separates me from God.

4. God sent Jesus to be the Savior of the world.

5. God sent Jesus to pay the price for my sin.

6. Jesus will never leave me.

7. When I trust in Jesus, God makes me his child.

8. God celebrates when I come back to him.

Bible Verses To Know For Older Children

Session 1
❑ Exodus 34:14 "You must worship no other gods, but only the LORD, for he is a God who is passionate about his relationship with you."

Session 2
❑ Romans 3:12 "All have turned away from God; all have gone wrong. No one does good, not even one."

Session 3
❑ Romans 3:23 "For all have sinned; all fall short of God's glorious standard."

❑ Romans 6:23 "For the wages of sin is death, but the free gift of God is eternal life through Christ Jesus our Lord."

Session 4
❑ John 14:6 "Jesus told him, 'I am the way, the truth, and the life. No one can come to the Father except through me.' "

Session 5
❑ Romans 3:25 "For God sent Jesus to take the punishment for our sins and to satisfy God's anger against us. We are made right with God when we believe that Jesus shed his blood, sacrificing his life for us. God was being entirely fair and just when he did not punish those who sinned in former times."

Session 6
❑ John 5:24 "I assure you, those who listen to my message and believe in God who sent me have eternal life. They will never be condemned for their sins, but they have already passed from death into life."

Session 7
❑ John 1:12 "But to all who believed him and accepted him, he gave the right to become children of God."

Big Words To Learn

HOLY

Perfect in every way; set apart for God; pure. God is holy.

MIRACLES

Wonderful things that only God can do. Jesus did many miracles to prove that he is God. For example, Jesus calmed a storm on the Sea of Galilee, he fed 5,000 people with a little boy's lunch, and he made blind people see.

PASSIONATE

Caring about something so much that we put all our thought and energy into it.

PROPHECY

Words that tell of something that will happen before it ever happens. Four hundred to five hundred years before Jesus was born, God led men to tell us facts about Jesus. These facts are prophecies.

RESURRECTION

To come back from the dead. Jesus died on the cross but three days later he came back to life. We say Jesus was resurrected when he came back to life.

SAVIOR

A person who rescues someone or something else. Jesus can rescue us from our sin. Jesus wants to be our Savior.

SIN

Choosing our own selfish way to live, and not choosing to live by God's rules.

SINS

The things we choose to say, do, or think which the Bible tells us are wrong and are against God's will, such as lying, cheating, and stealing.

THE WORLD

When we say "the world's Big Lie," we are using the word world to mean most of the people around us. In Lesson One we learn that most people (the world) do not think they need a friendship with God.

The Big Truths

Session 1
God created me to be his friend.

Stand up and clasp hands together, like a hand shake.

Session 2
God is holy and takes my sin seriously.

Use arms and hands to make an X across the face.

Session 3
Sin separates me from God.

With arms extended forward in front of their body, hands flexed with fingers pointed upward, take two steps back..

Session 4
God sent Jesus to be the Savior of the world.

Touch palm of right hand with the middle finger of left hand, then repeat the gesture with opposite hands, as in the sign language symbol for Jesus, and point to heaven.

Session 5
God planned for Jesus to pay the price for my sins.

Cross hands over face again as in Truth 2; but then break arms apart and reach up to God like a child who wants to be held reaches up to his father.

Session 6
Jesus will never leave me.

Hug yourself with arms wrapped around body.

Session 7
When I trust in Jesus, God makes me his child.

Form arms as if rocking a baby.

Session 8
God celebrates when I come back to him.

Begin by clapping hands then raise arms, palms up and hands raised to God.